# Are Organized Sports Better for Kids Than Pickup Games?

YES!

*Kathleen McAlpin Blasi*

MONDO

As I wrote this book, I had many conversations with adults and kids alike—too numerous to mention individually—who are nostalgic and passionate about sports and games. Thank you for contributing to the authenticity and spirit of this book.

I dedicate this book to Frank, Meg, and Marie—my favorite athletes and pickup pals.

—K.M.B.

Text copyright © 2007 by Kathleen McAlpin Blasi

Photo credits:

Yes! Cover: © Royalty-Free/CORBIS, © Royalty-Free/CORBIS; p.4: Flying Colours Ltd./ Digital Vision/Getty Images; p.9: Lori Adamski Peek/Stone/Getty Images; p.11: Getty Images Sport; p. 13:© Ariel Skelley/CORBIS; p. 15:© Eric O'connell/Taxi/Getty Images; p. 16: © B Busco/Photographer's Choice/Getty Images; p. 18: © David Madison/Stone/ Getty Images; p. 21: ©Stephanie Weiler/zefa/CORBIS

No! Cover: © Royalty-Free/CORBIS, © Royalty-Free/CORBIS; p. 5: © Vicky Kasala/ Photodisc Red/Getty Images; p. 6: © Loungepark/Photonica/Getty Images; p. 8: Getty Images Sport; p.9: © Yellow Dog Productions/The Image Bank/Getty Images; p. 12: © Cohen/Ostrow/Digital Vision/Getty Images; p. 14: © Scott Indermaur Photography LLC/ Workbook stock/Getty Images; p. 17: © Purestock/Getty Images; p. 18: © Rubberball Productions/Getty Images; p. 20: © photo & co./Taxi/Getty Images; p.22 & 23: © joSon/ Taxi/Getty Images

For information contact:

MONDO Publishing
980 Avenue of the Americas
New York, NY 10018

Visit our website at www.mondopub.com

Printed in China

08 09 10 11   9 8 7 6 5 4 3 2

ISBN 1-59336-765-1

Designed by Witz End Design

# Contents

| | | |
|---|---|---|
| **Introduction** | What are organized sports, and why are they better than pickup games? | 4 |
| **Argument 1** | Organized sports help kids get regular exercise. | 6 |
| **Argument 2** | In organized sports, young athletes get to learn from the pros. | 8 |
| **Argument 3** | Physical Education is a form of organized sports that can lead to a lifetime love of physical activity. | 10 |
| **Argument 4** | Adapted Physical Education is a form of organized sports that allows kids with disabilities to fully participate. | 12 |
| **Argument 5** | Organized sports are important for mental health. | 14 |
| **Argument 6** | Organized sports help kids avoid risky behavior. | 16 |
| **Argument 7** | Organized sports help kids form friendships and foster camaraderie. | 18 |
| **Argument 8** | Organized sports can lead to careers in professional sports. | 19 |
| **Argument 9** | Organized sports prepare kids for the real world. | 20 |
| **Conclusion** | Benefits abound in organized sports! | 22 |
| **Time Line** | Organized Youth Sports in America | 23 |
| **Glossary** | | Pages with the purple border |

## *What are organized sports, and why are they better than pickup games?*

A coach blows a whistle, and players gather for a pre-game pep talk. Bleachers and portable chairs on the sidelines creak as spectators greet each other and settle in. Uniforms streak by in a rainbow of color. On fields and courts across America, a new sports season has begun.

According to the National Council of Youth Sports, more than 40 million kids in the United States play organized youth sports such as hockey, baseball, soccer, or football. Unlike pickup games, organized sports operate under specific rules and regulations. Formal teams are made up of a designated number of players, and there is usually at least one adult who acts as a coach.

Organized youth sports have certainly become a part of American culture. One of the first organized youth sports programs began in 1939

**Play ball!**

when Carl Stotz of Williamsport, Pennsylvania, founded Little League Baseball. Today Little League is the largest organized youth sports program in the world. In addition to baseball, countless choices are now available to kids who want to participate in organized sports.

In previous decades, pickup games were more common than they are today. Groups of kids could just get a ball and spend hours exercising and playing on neighborhood streets and sandlots. However, changes in American society have led to a decline in these outdoor free-play activities. Land development has decreased the amount of open space, thereby reducing the number of places where kids can play. Today's news reports of violence, particularly regarding crimes against young people, have many parents and guardians frightened to the point that they won't send their kids outside to play unsupervised. Further, passive activities that didn't exist decades ago, such as watching television, playing video games, and using computers, compete for children's time—time that could be spent on physical activity. All these changes have spurred a growing demand for ways that young people can take part in physical activities in structured, supervised environments. Organized youth sports — which provide adult supervision, safety equipment, regular exercise, and family fun— successfully meet this demand and offer a solution to the many challenges kids and parents face in the 21st century.

The following pages detail some reasons why organized sports are the best way to provide young people with the physical activity they need— more so than informal "pickup games."

## *Organized sports help kids get regular exercise.*

Many years ago, people *had* to be physically active in order to survive. At various points in history, people had to hunt, chop wood, plow fields, carry water, operate a hand loom—the list goes on and on. Eventually machines came along to make the tasks easier, but even the machines required human effort and sometimes a lot of strength to run. For example, an "iron" used to iron clothing was just that—a block of iron. Most kinds of employment involved some type of physical labor. Without cars, people walked to work and to school.

Today our lifestyles are much more sedentary. We drive or take the bus to most of our destinations, because the place we are going is too far away or we have to be there in a hurry. Research shows that more than nine million kids, ages 6 to 11, are overweight or obese—four times more than the numbers in the 1960s and 1970s. Childhood obesity is an increasing problem. Young people and adults spend much more time at passive activities than in the past. For instance, kids use computers, watch hours of television, and play video games to the point of injuring the muscles in their hands! The American Heart Association states, "kids who consistently spend more than ten hours a week watching TV, sitting at the computer, or playing video games will probably end up overweight."

Organized sports are the perfect antidote to such passive activities. According to Dr. Gail Saltz of New York Presbyterian Hospital, kids should spend no more than one to two hours per day in front of TV and computer screens. They should devote at least as much time to physical activity as they do to "screen time."

*When Jason went home after school there wasn't much to do except finish his homework, mess around on the computer, and watch TV. He would have liked to play outside, but his family's backyard wasn't very big and there weren't really any other kids on his street. "It was pretty boring," Jason says.*

*"Then at school the principal announced they were going to start an after-school track and field program. My parents signed me up and now three days a week, I get to do all these cool sports—like running relay races. I'm not the fastest one on my team, but my stamina's getting a lot better. Maybe when I start high school, I'll try out for cross country."*

Physical activity is important because it builds stamina as well as healthy bones and muscles. It helps to reduce body fat and controls weight. Exercising decreases the risk of heart disease, cancer, and high blood pressure—diseases that can set in later in life. When hearts and lungs are out of shape, they have to work harder. Exercise helps them to work efficiently.

Kids who participate in organized youth sports (thereby getting regular physical activity) are more likely to become healthy, active adults who value fitness. In contrast, kids who play pickup sports do so on a whim. As there is no set schedule, they might not get enough exercise to ensure a healthy lifestyle.

Get UP

Get out

Get active!

# Argument 2

## *In organized sports, young athletes get to learn from the pros.*

Organized sports programs depend on coaches to provide kids with knowledge of the sport, to build their enthusiasm for athletics, and to protect players' safety. They also serve as important role models.

Coaches are experienced, and they know how to teach. What better way to learn a sport than from someone who really knows how to play? A coach can teach the specialized techniques that players need in order to excel. And they can pass on their enthusiasm for teamwork and the competitive spirit.

> "If I've done my job as a teacher in practice, then at the games I'm just a spectator."
>
> Ed
> *Soccer Coach,*
> *Elite Girls Program*

*One dad values physical activity and began coaching in order to get his daughter to participate in soccer. Today, eight years later, she is in junior high school and participates in several different sports. Her dad is still her soccer coach. Why?*

"*Coaching gives me an opportunity to spend time with my kids. I like to see all the players develop, too. I also enjoy competition and being part of a team. Planning practices and seeing the players execute plays based on those practices is very rewarding.*"

Coaches also know how to create a safe setting in which to play and learn. In pickup games, there are no adults present to provide such guidance. Kids risk injury if they perform skills incorrectly, use the wrong equipment, or push themselves too far. For example, a group of young kids playing pickup baseball might decide they want to play like the pros and use a hardball. Without helmets or proper safety precautions, one wild pitch with a hardball can lead to someone being knocked out.

In addition, coaches have the capability to teach more complicated skills that are needed for a particular sport. For example, kids might be able to learn to dribble a soccer ball on their own, but a coach who has training and experience can teach kids to properly "head" (use their head to hit) a soccer ball. This is an advanced soccer skill, and if players don't perform it correctly, they might miss the ball or hit it with the wrong part of their heads and get hurt.

Another way coaches help kids learn a sport is by making it fun. Sometimes players have such a good time that they don't realize they're learning an important skill.

*Six-year-old Andre looks forward to soccer practice. His creative coach uses silly games, like "Coneheads," to remind the players to keep the ball close and look up while dribbling.*

*"I put a cone on my head," giggles Andre. "Then I dribble the ball and try to keep the cone on my head. It's really fun!"*

Lastly, coaches serve as role models. In organized sports, a coach's reaction to mistakes is important. If the coach teaches players to learn from mistakes, instead of becoming discouraged when making them, players will focus on what they learned and on what they might do differently the next time. When a team loses, the coach helps players to keep the loss in perspective. Left to their own devices, kids might sulk after a loss or blame others.

This girl has learned from her coach to look up when dribbling.

## *Physical Education is a form of organized sports that can lead to a lifetime love of physical activity.*

One form of organized youth sports is physical education (PE), which is part of the school curriculum. PE is a kind of sampler—kids get a chance to try a wide variety of sports from gymnastics to martial arts to volleyball and beyond. Often PE introduces kids to sports they might otherwise not have known about.

PE can spark an interest in sports that can last a lifetime. Since PE students are exposed to a broad range of sports and activities, kids can choose which sports they might like to try outside of school. For example, after being exposed to both tennis and track in PE, a kid might decide that tennis isn't really for him, but that he really enjoys track. This discovery might lead him to try out for the track team at the next opportunity.

*Ron Whitcomb, Athletic Director of Victor Central Schools in Upstate New York, says that his district's primary goal is to help kids be active for life. "The district's goal is not to produce professional athletes; rather, it is to encourage a love of fitness."*

*Mission accomplished. Michelle, a former Victor student, is currently enrolled as a college outdoor recreation major. She is working toward a certificate in Physical Education. She gives credit for her decision to her former school, where in PE, she was given the chance to try many different athletic activities. Michelle had a positive experience with organized sports and has chosen to base her career on that.*

Spike!

PE during the school day is a great way to make sure that all kids—not just athletes—get exercise. For kids who don't participate in sports outside of school, PE may be their only major physical activity.

PE is considered so important that it's endorsed by the federal government. In 1972 a law called Title IX was passed. This law requires educational institutions that receive any money from the U.S. government to spend as much on girls' and women's programs (including physical education) as they do on boys' and men's. In addition, the U.S. government also sponsors a program called the Carol M. White Physical Education Program (PEP) which is designed to fund PE classes. Several professional athletes, including National Football League quarterback Peyton Manning and Olympic basketball star Jennifer Azzi, have spoken in support of expanding this program.

"Our schools are the best place to reach all our children."

Peyton Manning
*National Football League quarterback*

# Argument 4

## *Adapted Physical Education is a form of organized sports that allows kids with disabilities to fully participate.*

For some kids, the physical education classes they take in school might be their sole means of physical activity. This can be particularly true of kids with disabilities. All the benefits of regular exercise discussed earlier apply to kids with physical challenges. They, too, reap the rewards of healthy hearts, bones, and muscles.

That is why schools provide adapted physical education (APE). According to the website PE Central, adapted physical education is defined as "physical education which may be adapted or modified to address the individualized needs of children and youth who have gross motor development delays." APE allows all kids, regardless of ability, to fully participate in physical education. Teachers customize lessons so that each student has a safe and successful class experience. Kids learn new skills and get to see what it's like to be a member of a team.

*Jim, an adapted physical education teacher, customizes his lessons to meet the needs of his students. One of them, Ryan, has a disease that slowly weakens his muscular coordination and affects his balance, speech, and eyesight. Ryan, laden with pads and a helmet, gets to play three-on-three floor hockey with his teacher and friends. He uses a hockey stick to both shoot the puck and to support himself.*

*As Ryan's condition changes, so do Jim's lesson plans. He places mats around the gym so that Ryan will be safe when he falls. When Ryan can no longer stand, Jim gives him a chair so*

> "Everything we do in class needs some sort of adaptation so Ryan can participate."
>
> Jim
> *adapted physical education teacher*

*that he can play sitting down. As Ryan's eyesight worsens, making it difficult for him to see a puck, Jim uses a ball instead. Ryan brings in his brother's old hockey equipment and pretends he's a professional hockey player. Through APE, Ryan is able to participate in his favorite sport, just like other kids.*

In contrast, pickup games cannot provide these special accommodations. A child like Ryan might be left out of pickup games because his physical abilities are less than those of the other kids. Other children also may not be sensitive to or even understand Ryan's special needs. Even if he did participate, a child like Ryan might not have the confidence to keep playing without a trained instructor to guide and protect him.

**This boy's wheelchair won't interfere with his getting a hit.**

# Argument 5

## *Organized sports are important for mental health.*

The physical benefits of organized sports are obvious, but exercise is also important for mental health. Participating in a sport—including trying something new and seeing your new skills grow—helps your sense of well-being. Through organized sports, young people gain a sense of accomplishment, which in turn results in self-confidence.

> According to the World Health Organization, regular physical activity "helps prevent and control feelings of anxiety and depression."

Coaches who encourage players and who offer constructive criticism contribute to kids' having a positive attitude. Kids experience great pride as they work hard and improve their skills. This self-confidence can promote leadership qualities.

*Kenny does well in school but is very shy. He seldom raises his hand in class. On those rare occasions when he does volunteer, his heart beats faster and he feels butterflies in his stomach.*

*But Kenny is a different person on the lacrosse field. He is a skilled, cooperative player. He has the respect of coaches and teammates alike. Kenny's self-confidence really becomes apparent when he develops a new play and shares it with his coach and teammates. The coach uses it in a game, and the players successfully execute it. Kenny is vocal on the field and cheers for his teammates when he is on the bench.*

*Kenny's teacher comes to watch a school game. "Is that Kenny? I barely recognize him!" the teacher beams. "Just look at him! To see this confident side of Kenny is to see him in a whole new light!"*

Spectators of an organized sport provide important encouragement as well. When players hear their fans—especially family members—root for them, it helps young players to feel good about themselves and inspires them to give the game their all. Even when the players make mistakes, if coaches, parents, and friends cheer them on, they know that mistakes are okay and that they can do better next time. Such positive reinforcement strongly nurtures kids' sense of self-worth.

In contrast, pickup games risk damaging kids' self-confidence. Without adults there to mediate disputes, kids might not be able to work out problems, which could spiral out of control. Shy or sensitive kids in particular might experience lowered self-esteem and be discouraged from participating in the future.

"It's miiiine!"

## *Organized sports help kids avoid risky behavior.*

A person with high self-esteem is more likely to make good choices. Youth who make poor choices can get themselves into trouble, even to the extent of breaking the law.

Organized sports offer an alternative to these risky choices. The first organized youth football league was actually formed in order to keep kids out of trouble. In Philadelphia in 1929, young boys made a pastime of throwing rocks at factory windows. Joseph J. Tomlin, a New York stockbroker who was a native of Philadelphia, founded the Junior Football Conference in response to this problem. Area businesses joined together to fund the athletic program that later became the Pop Warner Conference. The kids in this organized sports program were kept so busy that they didn't have time to even think about getting into trouble!

Today in many schools, student athletes sign contracts in which they promise to maintain good grades and proper behavior. If a player does not honor the contract, he or she cannot play on the team.

Organized sports keep kids happy, active, and focused.

Latoya, an avid basketball player and fan, grew up with many challenges. Her parents both died when she was very young. During Latoya's freshman year of high school, varsity basketball coach Scott Smith had his sights set on bringing her up to play on his team. But Latoya violated her school's rules and thus her student-athlete contract, which led to a two-game suspension from the freshman team. But coach Smith didn't give up on her. He recognized her ability and told her that she could be successful if she made a commitment to the sport and honored her student-athlete contract.

Through hard work, Latoya found success in both the classroom and on the basketball court. Her love of the game provided her with excellent motivation to maintain good grades. Latoya played varsity basketball in her sophomore year, and in her senior year, she was named captain and led her team to a state championship.

"I never was a student who had great grades," says Latoya. "Basketball taught me to care about my future and to take responsibility for meeting goals I never thought I could achieve. Basketball also allows me to clear my head when times are hard, to just do something I love and forget about all the negatives."

Today Latoya is a sophomore at a junior college. She plans to become a physical education teacher. She has a good chance to be awarded an athletic scholarship to a four-year school.

## *Organized sports help kids form friendships and foster camaraderie.*

Part of the fun of sports is socializing, learning to get along with others, and forming friendships. In the spirit of cooperation, organized sports help kids to gain social skills and to contribute as members of a team. Whether players are actively participating in a game or sitting on the bench for the time being, they benefit from the social side of sports. Through practices and games, kids make friends as they define their roles on teams. Often the more sports kids play, the wider their circle of friends. Each exposure to a new sport or team presents the chance to meet people and establish a rapport with them. These friendships can be lasting, since they are based on a shared love of the sport.

While it is possible to make friends and establish camaraderie playing pickup games, too, organized sports provide a ready-made structure for building new friendships in many different settings. All you have to do is sign up and show up.

*Kara's family has to move a lot, because of her father's job. "Every couple of years, we move to a different place, and I have to make friends all over again," she says. "It's hard." One thing that makes it a little less difficult is soccer. Kara has been playing for several years—so wherever her family moves, the first thing her parents do is sign her up with an organized soccer league.*

*"It's almost like soccer is my 'home.' No matter what city I'm in, I start to feel okay as soon as I get on a team and we're on the field. Also I'm a pretty good player—and I cheer a lot when I'm on the bench. It's easier making new friends when you help your team win!"*

These girls can't wait
to start playing!

18

## *Organized sports can lead to careers in professional sports.*

For a select few, organized youth sports are a path to a professional career. With the help of good teachers and coaches, a strong commitment to a sport, and lots of hard work, kids might use their organized sports experience as a stepping stone to a spot on a professional team. However, even if hard work doesn't lead to professional status, players still reap the rewards of practice, dedication, and effort, all of which are skills that will serve them well for their entire lives.

*Diana Taurasi, a professional basketball player, began playing the game when she was in second grade. By the time she reached sixth grade, she was better than most of the boys and girls in her California town.*

*Diana began playing more competitive ball in seventh grade and by her sophomore year in high school, she was signing autographs! Spectators packed the gyms to see her play.*

*After high school, Diana attended the University of Connecticut, where she led their team, the UConn Huskies, to three straight national titles. Her college career brought her two Naismith College Player of the Year awards. This award is given annually to college basketball's top male and female players.*

*Diana Taurasi's involvement and success in organized youth sports led to her becoming a college sports star. From college basketball, she went on to represent the United States in the 2004 Summer Olympics, where her team won the gold medal. Her sports career reached its height when she was selected to play professionally for the Phoenix Mercury (one of the teams in the Women's National Basketball Association [WNBA]).*

# Argument 9

## Organized sports prepare kids for the real world.

Organized youth sports help prepare kids for the challenges of the real world. The skills and life lessons they acquire will be used in many situations throughout childhood, adolescence, and adulthood.

Organized sports teach accountability. Teammates rely on each other to fulfill their obligations to the team and to be responsible for what they have agreed to do and are expected to do. For example, team members must have their equipment ready, show up on time, and try their best. Being prepared, punctual, and putting forth one's best effort are skills that players will use for the rest of their lives.

Organized sports teach fair play. Teammates must take turns, share playing time, and work out problems. Organized sports are a great way to teach kids that they must follow the rules of the game and that there are penalties for not doing so. For example, in the game of soccer, if you kick the ball out of bounds, the other team gets possession of the ball. Pickup games, which do not have the same kinds of rules, do not similarly prepare kids for the real world.

Very young children think in terms of what is best for themselves, not necessarily what is fair. As kids get older, organized sports help them to consider others' points of view. Life, for kids and adults alike, requires treating people fairly. Rules are a part of life, whether one's on the playing field, in the classroom, on the job, or driving a car.

*Nine-year-old Max, a baseball player, remembers a lesson in fairness.*

*"I was psyched when we were finally old enough to pitch, instead of the coaches pitching to us. I liked being such an important player on my team. But I was mad when my turn to pitch was over."*

*Max had pitched two innings. He was then re-assigned to play left field. Max was upset. "Coach," he complained, "I thought I was the pitcher!"*

*"You were, Max, but now it's Tom's turn to pitch. Go ahead, guy, take the field."*

*Max was sure the coach had not liked his pitching, but he was relieved when he found out later that the rules of the league allow players to pitch no more than two innings.*

Organized sports encourage teamwork. Each member of a team is assigned a position and must fulfill the duties of that position. All positions work together to achieve a common goal, such as scoring a point, crossing the finish line, improving skills, or winning. By learning to work in a group, kids discover that it is often easier to attain a goal by working with others than by working alone.

Organized sports teach personal discipline. In the face of making mistakes, players must have the tenacity to try again and not give up. Also, belonging to a team sometimes requires sacrifice, such as declining a sleepover invitation the night before a game. Athletes need plenty of rest in order to give their top performance. Organized youth sports require what the real world does—the ability to give up something for the sake of gaining something else and the ability to persevere.

These soccer players are collaborating nicely and enjoying themselves at the same time.

*According to Joe Altobelli, former professional baseball player, coach, and manager, there's a phrase used in baseball: If you play baseball, you eat a lot of humble pie. "A good hitter only has to be successful 30 percent of the time," says Altobelli. "That means that for every ten times you're at bat, you only have to get three hits. Sounds easy, right? But what's important to remember is that what makes you get those three hits is how you handle the seven outs."*

# Conclusion

## *Benefits abound in organized sports!*

Benefits abound in organized youth sports. They range from fun and fitness to learning how to interact in the real world. Through organized sports, kids can engage in an active lifestyle while playing in a safe environment. Their bodies benefit from developing strong bones, muscles, hearts, and lungs. Organized sports participants learn from experienced adults who offer teaching and encouragement. Taking part in organized sports helps kids to develop self-confidence, accountability, personal discipline, and a lifelong love of physical fitness.

Each day in towns across the United States, whistles blow and buzzers sound, signaling the end of a game. Chairs are folded, and duffel bags zipped closed. Bleachers creak as spectators rise. Adults and kids cheer and give high-fives. For now the game is over—until kids, parents, and coaches meet again in the fun, spirited competition of organized sports.

It's the very fact that these sports are *organized* that makes them ultimately better for kids than pickup games. While pickup games provide lots of fun and plenty of exercise and socializing, organized sports go way beyond that to open doors to the future for many talented kids, to teach life skills involving rules and teamwork, and in many cases to make allowances for kids whose level of participation needs to be monitored and adapted. Organized sports *are* better for kids than pickup games!

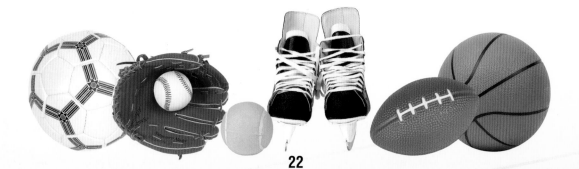

# Time Line of Organized Youth Sports in America

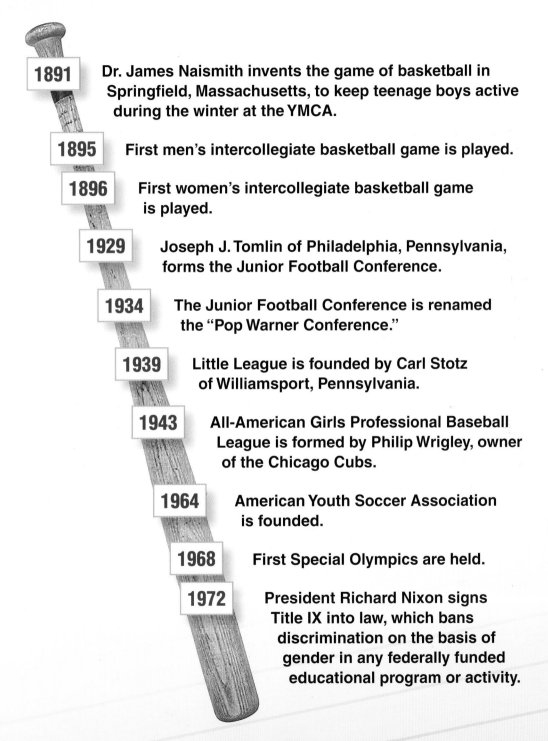

**1891** — Dr. James Naismith invents the game of basketball in Springfield, Massachusetts, to keep teenage boys active during the winter at the YMCA.

**1895** — First men's intercollegiate basketball game is played.

**1896** — First women's intercollegiate basketball game is played.

**1929** — Joseph J. Tomlin of Philadelphia, Pennsylvania, forms the Junior Football Conference.

**1934** — The Junior Football Conference is renamed the "Pop Warner Conference."

**1939** — Little League is founded by Carl Stotz of Williamsport, Pennsylvania.

**1943** — All-American Girls Professional Baseball League is formed by Philip Wrigley, owner of the Chicago Cubs.

**1964** — American Youth Soccer Association is founded.

**1968** — First Special Olympics are held.

**1972** — President Richard Nixon signs Title IX into law, which bans discrimination on the basis of gender in any federally funded educational program or activity.

# Are Organized Sports Better for Kids Than Pickup Games?

*Kathleen McAlpin Blasi*

# Contents

| Introduction | What are pickup games, and why are they better than organized sports? | 4 |
|---|---|---|
| Argument 1 | Pickup games are fun. | 6 |
| Argument 2 | Pickup games help kids to develop athletically. | 7 |
| Argument 3 | Pickup games allow anyone to play. | 9 |
| Argument 4 | Pickup games are kid-directed. | 11 |
| Argument 5 | In pickup games, kids learn by doing. | 13 |
| Argument 6 | Pickup games encourage kids to be creative. | 15 |
| Argument 7 | Pickup games foster leadership skills. | 16 |
| Argument 8 | Pickup games provide variety. | 17 |
| Argument 9 | Pickup games teach problem solving, listening skills, and tolerance. | 19 |
| Conclusion | Reap the benefits of pickup games! | 21 |
| Sample Pickup Games | Feel free to bend the rules. | 22 |
| Glossary | | Pages with the purple border |

# Introduction

## *What are pickup games, and why are they better than organized sports?*

The doorbell rings, and a neighborhood kid says, "Can you come out to play?" There's no need to ask, "Play what?" or "Where?" or "What time?" Grab a ball (any kind). Grab a glove and a bat or a hockey stick. Better yet, grab them all. No referee, no coach, no spectators. There are no age limits and no schedule. It's time for pickup games!

"Pickup," "backyard," "sandlot," and "free play" are all terms used to describe non-organized sports. The word "pickup" indicates the natural, spontaneous quality associated with non-organized sports. This type of play is free-form, kid-directed, and often competitive. There is no official playing field—a backyard, sandlot, city sidewalk, quiet street, or front stoop will do fine.

Pickup games have been around for hundreds of years. Native Americans played games involving running and archery. Children in Colonial times played leapfrog and hoop rolling (using a stick to propel a hoop, often made of wood, through fields and around town). Resourceful pioneer children played catch with an inflated pig bladder! In contrast, organized youth sports became part of American culture relatively recently—football in 1929 and Little League Baseball in 1939, to name two examples.

Organized sports are played on a set schedule. Practice sessions and games take place at particular times. They are headed up by an adult coach and are held on playing fields and in gymnasiums. There are time limits and time commitments, which sometimes overlap with family time. Organized sports also cost money. Players have to buy equipment and pay team or league fees for things such as renting field space.

Pickup games, however, which are still played today in neighborhoods and streets across America, are dependent simply on willing participants who have the time and space to strike up a game. Several different types of games can be played in a single day, or the entire day's play may involve just one game. And here's an interesting question: What is one thing that organized sports have that pickup games do not? *Adults.* Pickup games are run by kids, and this leads to creative play that fosters independence.

Read on to learn why pickup games are more beneficial to their players than organized youth sports.

These brothers are enjoying a winter game of leapfrog.

## *Pickup games are fun.*

The number one reason young people play pickup games is to have fun. Kids enjoy competing with one another. Competition allows kids to push themselves and hone their skills. Pickup games are also fun because kids are able to play without pressure from well-meaning adults. Pickup competition can be sprinkled with well-deserved and self-timed breaks that include having a snack, lying down on the grass, and sitting with friends to share the latest jokes. The kids decide when it's time to resume competition. Without pressure from coaches or other adults, players can feel free to enjoy being with friends, try out new skills, or push themselves to exceed a personal best.

*Seven-year-old Sophia recalls moving to her neighborhood. "It was summer. I remember because my mom wanted us to move before the school year started, so we could get to know the kids who lived around us. One of the first mornings in our new house, while I was still in bed, the doorbell rang. I heard my mom talking with someone at the front door. I got out of bed and headed downstairs.*

*"There was a girl about my age. She was so excited she was hopping up and down. 'Do you want to come outside and play?' she asked. 'Sure,' I said. By the time I got dressed, put on my shoes, and went outside, there must have been ten other kids hanging around.*

*"That day and almost every other day that summer, my brother and I woke up early. We went out to play whatever game we felt like playing that day—Fort Knox, whiffle ball, touch football, Kick the Can. You name it!*

*"We couldn't get enough of playing with our friends. That summer was so much fun! And so was the one after that, and the one after that…"*

Twirling hoops is a great way to have some outdoor fun.

6

## *Pickup games help kids to develop athletically.*

Participating in pickup games helps kids to develop athletic skills. You don't need to be a member of a formal team to shoot baskets, play street hockey, or hit a tennis ball with a friend on the driveway. Kids who play pickup games develop better coordination and strengthen their muscles. Given their varied nature, pickup games can produce athletically well-rounded kids. For example, swimming and running help build endurance, while jump-rope games develop balance and coordination.

*Former professional baseball player, coach, and manager Joe Altobelli learned to play ball on the streets of Detroit. He batted with a broom handle and eventually honed his skills to the degree that he developed "quickness." According to Altobelli, "Quickness doesn't mean speed. It doesn't mean you run real fast. It's agility. Your brain is telling your whole body what to do. If your brain gets lazy, you lose that quickness and agility."*

*Prestigious colleges offered scholarships to Altobelli—the boy who learned to bat with a broom. He began playing professionally for the Cleveland Indians and enjoyed a long career that included coaching the New York Yankees and managing the Baltimore Orioles.*

Today's Major League Baseball rosters are full of the names of players who learned to play ball on the streets. Pickup games may lack uniforms and even some of the official equipment, but they contain the most important ingredient of all: a desire to play.

Professional baseball player Manuel Aristides Ramirez played ball with his dad in his homeland—the Dominican Republic. There he began to dream of becoming a big-league player. When he was 13 years old, Manny and his family moved to New York City.

Playing ball on the city streets, Manny's passion for baseball grew. Any chance he had, he participated in pickup games. Armed with a broomstick and sponge ball, he could bit farther than all the other kids. Manny Ramirez's experience playing in pickup games as a teenager helped him to develop his natural abilities and the talents that have made him a great baseball player.

Manny Ramirez, who got his start playing ball on the street with his pals, is considered one of the best all-around hitters in the major leagues.

# Argument 3

## *Pickup games allow anyone to play.*

Pickup games are for anyone who chooses to participate. There's no place for bench warming because kids determine who will do what. In organized sports, a coach has the final say about the number of games kids will play, who will play which positions, and how long each player remains in the game. In pickup games, kids determine playing time and even the rules. All kids need to do in order to play is show up.

Pickup games can be the first exposure to sports for some kids. As they get older, they might join organized youth sports teams, too, something they might not have done if they weren't initially exposed to pickup games. And while organized leagues might be a great choice for some kids, they don't work out for everyone. Unlike pickup games, organized leagues often hold tryouts, which means not all kids are chosen to participate.

The requirements for getting on an organized sports team get tougher as kids reach middle school and high school. Gifted players are chosen for a team, and the amount they are allowed to participate is based on their skill levels (as well as attendance at practices and abiding by school rules). If players with average skills aren't actually cut at tryouts, they might be sidelined, or kept on the bench, waiting to be called to play.

However, when players are stuck on the bench they become more spectators than participants. These team members might feel their worth to the team is diminished. This often results in players dropping out of, or being dropped from, organized sports.

Bored football players slump on the sidelines, a familiar sight in organized sports.

In pickup games, there are no cuts. Everyone makes the team, regardless of skill level or age. Through free play, kids have a great opportunity to stay physically fit and to socialize, without the pressure and disappointment sometimes associated with organized sports.

*Paul began playing organized sports when he was seven years old. When he reached seventh grade, he decided to try out for a school team. He was cut. He tried out in eighth grade. He was cut again, but the coach predicted he would make it in ninth grade. The coach's prediction did not come true.*

*Discouraged but not defeated, Paul invented his own sport with his own league. He invited several friends over to his house to play "swimming pool whiffle ball." It caught on. The boys kept score, developed league standings, and recorded statistics.*

*"I watched from the kitchen window," recalls Paul's father. "It was a scene of pure joy. To see our son recover from the disappointment of being cut from the school team—to see him rise to the challenge of making his own competitive fun—gave us great satisfaction."*

*Paul is a sophomore in college now. Last summer he gathered his old team together for a friendly game of swimming pool whiffle ball. And he predicts he will do so this summer as well.*

# Argument 4

## *Pickup games are kid-directed.*

Competition is good, as long as no one is hurt in the process. In pickup games, kids decide what's at stake, whether their game will be friendly and scoreless or as competitive as an Olympic event. Pickup games are an excellent alternative to organized sports, where competition can be fierce and the pressure extreme.

In organized sports, while it's natural for emotions to run high, well-meaning adults can sometimes get carried away. Parents might yell at coaches and officials, or worse, at the young players. Sometimes adults lose sight of why kids play sports to begin with—to have *fun*. Parents who push too hard might think they are helping their children to excel in a given sport, but they could actually be doing more harm than good. Kids who are pressured too much will not enjoy playing; instead they might come to see sports as a source of frustration.

Parents are not the only guilty parties when their kids play organized sports; sometimes coaches, too, lose sight of why kids play. If coaches subscribe to a win-at-all-costs philosophy, this might benefit them personally, but it does not benefit those who matter most—the players.

> On organized sports . . .
>
> "When parents start telling us what to do, it can be the opposite of what the coach is telling us to do. It's confusing!"
>
> Kevin
> *10-year-old travel soccer player*

*Mike, father of a ten-year-old football player, struggles with how the coach structures his son's team. "His only goal is to win," Mike laments. "In the beginning of the season, he claimed that his goal was to develop these young boys into better football players, which would help them develop into better young men and even better citizens." "Well, that was just a lot of talk. He plays only the best players. The other four or five players are substitutes. They get the minimum number of plays as defined by the league."*

No adults, please! These kids set out on their bikes for an afternoon of adventure.

Lack of playing time will not develop players in any sport. Kids hit their athletic strides at different ages. The kid on the bench today may have the potential to someday be a great athlete.

Kids who play pickup games are self-starters and often highly motivated. Their participation is not dependent on an end-of-year trophy or adult approval. Pickup games are kid-driven. That means low-key kids can play a low-key game, while more competitive kids can get as much playing time as they want. Kids call the shots, and that's good for them.

# Argument 5

## *In pickup games, kids learn by doing.*

In pickup games, experience and peers—rather than a coach—are the teachers. Players make mistakes, which are great opportunities to learn. Sometimes the lessons that stick best are those that involve a lot of trial and error—without anyone looking over your shoulder.

Consider writers. Aspiring writers can read all kinds of books on writing. They can take classes on writing. They can meet writers and ask them questions. But to actually learn to be good writers, they need to (you guessed it!) *write*. Good writers are not born that way. They practice and make mistakes. And the more they write, the better they become. They learn by doing.

Similarly, when it comes to pickup games, kids learn by doing. They practice and make mistakes without worrying about competition or adults' reactions. This is the best way for kids to learn.

For example, in the game of soccer, kicking is an essential skill. Consider these two scenarios for learning it:

A coach describes how to kick a ball and explains the reasons why proper technique works. He draws a picture on his white board and then demonstrates. At this point, the player is not yet actively engaged in learning how to kick.

**OR**

A player kicks with her toe. The ball launches to the left. She tries again. This time, the ball veers to the right. She keeps trying, using different parts of her foot. She discovers on her own that kicking with the inside of her foot yields the best result. She isn't told what will or could happen. She does it and sees for herself.

*Maria's friends have asked her to go with them to a summer basketball camp. "I just want to relax," she tells them. "I don't want to go to any camps." Does this mean that Maria dislikes the game of basketball? Not at all. Maria prefers to shoot hoops in her driveway, something she can do anytime, either alone or with friends and family. She shoots over and over. When she plays Pig, Horse, and 21, which are variations on the game of basketball, she learns to sink baskets from different distances and angles. She is learning by doing, on her own terms and without the pressure of being tested or forced to compete. She spends as much or as little time practicing as she likes.*

*When her friends come back from basketball camp, Maria may even beat them at a friendly pickup game!*

**Will he make the shot? Friendly games with a neighbor will provide plenty of opportunities for this boy to perfect his technique.**

## *Pickup games encourage kids to be creative.*

Pickup games present opportunities for kids to be creative. To strike up a game, it's not necessary to have all the proper equipment or the money to purchase it. With a little imagination, unconventional equipment will do just fine. In addition, there are no adults with handbooks and rosters. Kids form teams and make their own rules. Although an existing sport might be the basis for a game, kids are free to create new rules to suit their needs.

Organized sports encourage conformity and may hinder kids' creativity. The very premise of organized sports—that they are played according to certain rules and regulations—does not promote the use of the imagination. Organized sports must be played within the parameters of designated locations, rigid rules, and specified time limits.

*Marco, now 68 years old, recalls playing a variety of games on the neighborhood field when he was growing up in Massachusetts. "Teams were picked" he says, "and I was sometimes chosen last, but I didn't care. I was just happy to be outside playing with my friends."*

*Marco left the house at 8 A.M. and didn't return until he was hungry. When he and his friends played baseball, sometimes the ball wasn't in the best condition. But that didn't stop them from having a game. As long as they had the remnants of a ball and some electrical tape to wrap it in, that was good enough. They used burlap sacks for bases, and if they didn't have enough players to have a right fielder, the team at bat wasn't allowed to hit the ball into right field. If they did, it was considered an automatic out. The kids legislated what was fair and what was not. And they improvised so that they could keep the game going no matter what.*

# Pickup games foster leadership skills.

In organized sports, coaches volunteer or are appointed. Kids do not have a say in who their coach is. Therefore, they have little ability to influence what coaches do. It's very different in pickup games. Without adults to enforce rules and provide guidance, kids learn to think for themselves and develop a sense of independence. One or two kids will usually emerge as leaders. Often these kids are able to work with others and enforce fairness without bullying.

In pickup games, kids usually choose the team captains. As a result, the captains' authority is generally respected by the players. After all, the very people who are being led have chosen their leaders! This can be likened to our democratic means of electing our president. People vote, and the candidate who receives the majority of electoral votes becomes our nation's leader. In pickup games, kids feel they have a voice instead of having a leader imposed on them. Captains then take turns choosing sides, which yields a natural balance of age and skill. Kids see the power of their decision making. Their choices have a direct impact on the quality of their play.

*Jill reflects fondly on summer days playing pickup games in her neighborhood. Dylan, her brother, was always chosen to be a captain, no matter what game they were playing. It wasn't because he was the best player or the oldest. Dylan was chosen because the other kids respected his judgment and sense of fairness.*

*"I was on the younger side and was always among the last picked when choosing sides," says Jill. "If Dylan picked me, he always high-fived me. I never sensed that he begrudged my age. Whatever we played, he gave me as much playing time as anyone else. I felt that I was an important part of the team.*

*"Now that I'm an adult, I understand that as a leader it's important that those under your care feel good about what they're doing. If they do, they will do a better job for you. Dylan figured that out a long time ago."*

*Dylan's diplomatic skills carried through to adulthood. He is now a respected leader in his community.*

## *Pickup games provide variety.*

If variety is the spice of life, then pickup games are red hot chili peppers. In pickup games, kids have a chance to play games they might not otherwise have an opportunity to experience. In contrast, if parents sign up kids for organized sports that require strict time commitments, kids might not have time to try other physical activities.

When kids get together in an unstructured situation, several different types of games can be played in the same day. For example, when kids get tired of playing football, they might turn to street hockey or go swimming. Variety produces well-rounded kids and helps them discover where their talents lie and what they enjoy.

Because pickup games are varied, they require that players exercise different muscle groups. They allow kids to experience a healthy range of activities rather than limiting themselves at a time in life when their bodies need to develop and grow. The American Academy of Pediatrics warns against specialization in sports at an early age because such specialization can lead to repetitive-motion injury. Consider the motion of pitching. A young person's bones and muscles are still growing. Working an isolated muscle group or joint over and over can cause damage.

Pickup games include countless variations of established sports, but they also include yard games like Spud and Capture the Flag. Sidewalk games are another type of pickup activity. Hopscotch and jump rope, for example, are sidewalk games that help kids develop balance and hand-eye coordination. And who knows? With the rhyming jingles that go along with some of these games, kids might develop their singing voices, too!

**Kids of all ages can participate in pickup games.**

Molly and her friends like to make up their own rules to games. "We're all really good at jump rope," she says, "so we try to make it harder!" Instead of saying jump rope rhymes, they turn the game into a math challenge. Every time it is someone's turn to jump, the jumper calls out a number from 2 to 9. Then the "turners" have to count the number of jumps in multiples of that number. If one of the turners makes a mistake, the jumper gets to choose their "fate," either ten jumping jacks or running around the yard three times. "Actually," Molly adds, "we keep adding new rules. That way, it's always fun and we never get tired of playing."

## *Pickup games teach problem solving, listening skills, and tolerance.*

Pickup games help kids develop problem-solving skills. The absence of adults makes it necessary for kids to solve their own problems. Kids determine what is fair and what isn't. They must directly interact and listen to one another—if they want the game to continue. With such a strong incentive, kids quickly learn the importance of fair play and speedy problem solving. To solve a dispute, kids might take a vote to bend a rule. Or they might make up a new one.

*Tasha, mother of four, reflects on watching her children interact with others while playing backyard sports when they were young.*

*"My favorite thing to do was listen to the kids because they always had a way of just working things out. You'd hear them bicker and barter about who was going to do what, but they just wanted to get the game going, so they figured it out.*

*"One day I watched as one of the boys who lived across the street shoved my younger son in the chest. It was all I could do to keep myself from running to his rescue. I knew he wasn't hurt, at least not physically. My older son told the other boy that if he was going to bully anyone, he could just go home. The boy, I imagine from hurt pride, turned to walk away, got halfway across the street, then turned around and came back. He didn't say anything, but he knew not to mess with my kids. I was proud.*

*"After all, if they couldn't work it out, they wouldn't play. And, to them, that wasn't an option."*

Pickup games also require listening skills. In organized sports, coaches offer instruction and guidance. In pickup games kids often coach one another. If they don't listen to each other, their skills won't improve, and unsettled issues could end a day of playing. When kids listen and cooperate with one another, the success is shared.

Lastly, pickup games help kids learn tolerance and embrace diversity. The age span and skill level in pickup games can be wide. Older children have the opportunity to be role models and mentors. Younger children have an opportunity to learn from someone they look up to. Kids gather from different types of families and backgrounds. They're of different genders, ages, races, and cultures. Personalities range from shy and mild to aggressive and bold. Because pickup games mirror the diversity found in society, they teach kids to negotiate and appreciate real-world differences among people.

# Conclusion

## *Reap the benefits of pickup games!*

Pickup games have long been valued in American culture. They are still played every day in streets, backyards, and playgrounds across the country. Kids gather to have fun, compete, exercise, and socialize. Without even realizing it, they are developing healthy bodies and minds. Activities are varied and creative, and most importantly they are determined by kids' wants and needs. Games are not taught, *per se*, but the lessons learned are priceless.

What we think of as games are really lessons kids can use throughout life—lessons learned without a teacher or coach! Through free play, kids learn how to cooperate with each other, solve problems, and interact with children of varying ages and backgrounds. Pickup games set kids on a path to becoming responsible, creative, productive, and independent adults.

It's not the setting sun that beckons kids home when they're playing pickup games. After all, some activities are just better suited for long shadows and nighttime play. The signal to end comes at dinnertime or shower time or bedtime. One never knows when the call to come in will be sounded. After all, that would require organization, and that's not a necessary ingredient in the recipe for a fun day of pickup games.

With all of these benefits, pickup games are much better for kids than organized sports. Pickup games embrace all willing players—there are no cuts. Unlike organized sports, kids play without competitive pressure, and without adults to make every decision for them. Kids are completely in charge. They are forced to be imaginative, creative problem solvers—on the spot. And they learn tolerance and diversity as they welcome all comers to join the fun. Organized sports, while valuable, just can't compete with that list of benefits.

## Sample Pickup Games—Feel Free to Bend the Rules.

### 21

Variation of basketball. Play begins at the free throw line (drawn with chalk, if necessary). Once players score their first free throw, they can rebound the other players' missed shots. Shots scored on rebounds are worth one point. When a point is scored, that player goes to the free throw line and shoots until missing a shot, accumulating two points for each successful free throw. The first player to reach 21 points wins. This requires some strategy, as scoring more than 21 automatically sets that player back to "0."

### Blooper Ball

Variation of baseball. Use a bat, but use a beach ball instead of a baseball. Rules regarding outs and strikes apply. The runner is out when he or she is tagged with the ball.

### Capture the Flag

Split a field or yard in two. Each team hides its flag in its own territory. The object is for each team to capture the other team's flag. If a player is tagged in "enemy" territory while attempting to capture the opposing team's flag, that player is "jailed" in a designated area and can be freed by a teammate's tagging her. Variation: Fort Knox.

## H-O-R-S-E

Variation of basketball. Player 1 shoots from anywhere in the court. If he misses, Player 2 may shoot from anywhere she wishes. But if Player 1 makes his shot, Player 2 must make the same shot. If Player 2 misses, she gets an "H" in the word "H-O-R-S-E." Player 3 then may shoot from anywhere on the court. But if Player 2 makes the shot made by Player 1, Player 3 must make the same shot, and so on. Shooting cycles back to Player 1, who may take a new shot. Players are eliminated from the game once they miss 5 shots, spelling "H-O-R-S-E."

## Kick the Can

A combination of tag, hide-and-seek, and Capture the Flag. Place a can or bucket in the middle of the playing area. One team hides and one team is "It." The "It" players cover their eyes and count to 100. They try to find and tag each of the hiding players. Players who are tagged are sent to a designated "jail" area, usually near the can. If an untagged player kicks the can, his captured teammates are set free. When the "It" team catches all the opposing players, it wins the round. The teams alternate between hiding and being "It."

## Kickball

Variation of baseball. Instead of a baseball, two teams of players use a playground ball. Their legs/feet are the "bats," and they use their hands to catch the ball. Each team is allowed three outs, like in baseball, but outs are made by the fielding team catching a ball in the air or by fielding it and throwing it at the "batter" and hitting him with it (from the shoulders, down). If the ball hits the ground before hitting the batter, he is safe.

## Newcomb

Variation of volleyball. One team throws the ball over the net. If the opponent catches the ball, that team gets a point. If he or she misses, the throwing team gets a point. Teams alternate between throwing and catching.

## Relay Sack Race

Divide two teams into two groups each. Half of each team stands at each end of the playing area. Participants place both legs in a sack or old pillowcase. One player from each team hops to the other end of the playing area. When she arrives and touches the hand of the next teammate, that player hops to the other end of the playing area, and so on. The team whose players first cross the finish line wins.

## Spud

Assign each player a number, and choose a player to be "It." All players gather in a circle around "It," who throws a playground ball in the air and yells out a number. Everyone runs away from the ball except the player whose number was called. This player—who becomes the new "It"—runs to the ball, catches it, and yells "Spud!" Everyone must stop running. "It" then throws the ball at the closest person. If "It" hits that person, that person gets an "S." If the person catches the ball, then "It" gets an "S." If the ball doesn't hit the intended target or is not caught by him or her, no one gets an "S," and play starts again with a new "It." The game continues until each player but one has the letters S-P-U-D. The game can be made easier by allowing "It" to take three or four giant steps toward the chosen target before throwing the ball.

## Whiffle Ball

A street version of baseball. Each person keeps his own score and gets points when batting. If fielders catch the ball, no points are scored. If fielders touch but don't catch the ball, the batter gets one point. If the batter clears the ball (no one touches it), he gets two points. Players rotate batting and fielding.

# Glossary

**adapted physical education (APE)**
A physical education program designed specifically for students with unique physical needs

**agility**
the ability to move quickly and easily

**American Academy of Pediatrics**
an organization that advocates for the optimal health of young people, from infants to young adults

**American Heart Association**
an organization whose mission it is to reduce disability and death from heart disease and stroke

**coach**
a person who is in charge of a sports team, who teaches and prepares strategies for play

**confidence**
a strong belief in one's own abilities

**cut**
to eliminate a potential team member during the tryout phase of forming a team

**obese**
extremely overweight

**positive reinforcement**
encouragement that often leads to good behaviors being repeated in the future

**sedentary**
accustomed to sitting; getting too little exercise

**self-esteem**
a feeling of self-worth

**specialization**
focusing solely on participation in one activity

**starter**
a player who competes in a game or race from the beginning

**travel teams**
sports teams that travel around within and outside of their regions in order to play other teams at a highly competitive level

24